Loving Memories

Loving Memories

A Collection by B.J. Barkley

B.J. Barkley

To order additional copies of this book, contact:
Xlibris
1-888-795-4274
www.Xlibris.com
Orders@Xlibris.com
801479

Contents

With God's Help

We really need you very much,
you seem to have a gentle touch
We can always find the things you say
That makes our heartaches go away.

You guide us as we walk the path
And show your mercy, not your wrath
And even when we need correction
We know you also give protection.

Your love for us you've always shown,
And through your word, you've made it known
That if, through faith, we endure strife
The prize will be eternal life.

So, please, help me to go your way,
And do your will day after day.
Show us your love that's good and pure,
And with your help, we shall endure.

The Butterfly

The Butterfly is a beautiful thing
As it glides about on wing
It catches the light of the morning sun
It fades away when the day is done

It is one of God's delights
A miracle of joyous flight
The light reflects on it's colorful wings
As it soars on the breeze in early spring

It flirts and flutters with lovely grace
And sometimes flies right up to your face
Then darts away without a care and disappears, we know not where.

Ladybird's Flowers

May is known as the month for flowers
Which supposedly comes from April showers
But now we know it was Ladybird
That loved them so, she put out the word
That in the future there would be
flowers galore for all to see.

She had them planted everywhere
She wanted the whole world to share
In the love she had for all the flowers
So she had them planted in banks and bowers
Now when you think of "Johnson's Day"
You'll think of her flowers in bright array.

April's Song

April is the time of year when spring is in the air,
The flowers bloom so beautifully and love everywhere.
You hear it in the birds sweet song and in the morning breeze,
The April song is borne along by soft winds in the trees.
You feel it in the new dawn's mist and when you touch the flowers,
When you're in love, the April song goes on and on for hours.
You see it nearly everywhere, the sun, the moon, the stars.
The April song is with you, no matter where you are.
You see it in the golden moon and in the starry skies,
But most of all you see it in your loved one's eyes.
And when your loved one's by your side with words so soft and sweet,
Then two hearts twine together to make the song complete.

Jehovah's Love

I bask in the glow of Jehovah's love
He sends to me from up above.
He gives me peace when I am sad,
And heals the hurts that I have had.
He picks me up when I am low
And walks with me where e'er I go.
He gives me hope when I am down
And changes to laughter every frown
He gives me the warmth of the Bible's word
and when I pray, I know it's heard.
And if I pray in harmony
To his will, He grants to me
The strength to plant his Kingdom's seed
And all the things I really need.

Autumn

I love autumn, when the leaves are red and brown
And the slightest breeze sends them swirling around.
The air is cool and crisp and clear
To me, it's the nicest time of year
The days are sunny and the nights are cool
It's so pleasant to sit by a quiet pool.
And dream about the things you've done
While basking in the autumn sun.
The cool of the night calms your fears
And turns the time back through the years
To when your love was bright and new
And the touch of his kiss was like morning dew.
Yes, it's sweet to dream of days gone by
While you sit under an autumn sky.

Jehovah's Kingdom

Jehovah is the only God, Creator of us all,
His servants meet together at the local Kingdom Hall.
Do you know him and of his plans for all of human kind?
If not, then come and meet with us his secrets you will find.
He is a kind and loving God, our prayers he fulfills.
The Bible is no mystery for those who do his will.
His people take no part in this world with all it's crime,
They're busy teaching others of a peaceful, happy time
When Jehovah's Kingdom reigns on earth
with no more crime and war,
We feel this great new Kingdom is well worth working for.
So, come and seek the paradise that mankind has in store,
For those who do the will of God, will live forevermore.

With Sympathy

You have my deepest sympathy
I know how much you cared.
But, now you must remember
All the good times that you shared.

And though your hear is heavy,
You know their imperfection
Will be done away with,
In the coming resurrection.

So, be happy in Jehovah
And assured in His words are true,
For in the earthly paradise
All things will be made new.

Our Example

Our God is gracious, strong and mild,
He treats us as a little child.
He calls to us that we may come
And learn from him about his son.

And how he came to show the way
To guide our footsteps day by day
And we should follow where he leads
And if we do, he fills our needs.

So always talk to God in prayer
When you're in need, you'll find him there
But also give him all your praise
And he'll be with you all your days.

Discipline

Take hold on discipline, don't let go.
Our lives depend on this, you know.
Listen to discipline and become wise
Our future on this most surely relies.

He sends this discipline from above
Because he promised those he loves
That he would teach them lovingly
If they would listen faithfully.

So receive this discipline that gives insight
And thus put up a gallant fight
Accept this discipline gracefully
And we can live eternally.

So Many

So many years
So many pains
So many losses
Too few gains.

So many heartaches
So many tears
Can make you strong
Or make you fear.

So many live
So many die
It's up to each one
You and I.

So live your life
As though each day
Were the last one
Come what may.

Promises

In the final part of these last days
Many people will surely go and say
Come to Jehovah's mountain and learn
The truth of his words and thus discern
The meaning of the words his dear son said
He even promised to raise the dead
And through his ransom sacrifice
He made possible a paradise
On Earth for all who do his will
He also promised their cup to fill
He said not to hunger for all these things
Like silver and gold and diamond rings
But put your hope in our Father above
And show your neighbor the meaning of love
If you keep your faith and our works alive
The end of this system you will surely survive.

What Payment

What to Jehovah will I repay?
Gratitude day after day.
How will I show that I really care?
By turning to him each day in prayer.
What do I have to thank him for?
For the knowledge and wisdom of what's in store.
Without the gift of Jehovah's word
The truth of his kingdom would not be heard.
Without his spirit to keep us strong
We'd stumble and fall amid the throng.
Without the sacrifice of his son
The way to life would not be won.
Despite the bleakness of these "Last Days"
We have so much deserving praise.
We know that Jehovah is without end,
And on nothing from us He depend.
So, what to Jehovah must our payment be?
Justice and love and modesty.

The One I Love

The one I love is quite a guy
His eyes are nearly black
And when I look at him and smile
he smiles at me right back.

He has the most beautiful smile
I think I've ever seen
And when he looks at me and smiles
I feel just like a Queen

His arms are strong when he holds me tight
And yet they're gentle too
He pulls my head down to his chest
And pets me when I'm blue

The one I love is so wonderful
The sweetest love I've had
Sometimes he is mischievous
But he's never really bad

The one I love, he seems so wise
And yet has little to say
He doesn't need to say a thing
To drive your cares away.

I don't stay sad when he's around
There's always much to do
The one I love is my grandson and he is only two.

To Appease

You were upset
Because you were wet
And I was half out of my mind.

It's a wonder
With all the thunder
That all I did was unwind.....
a little

So come back to work
Forgive this jerk
You know I don't mean to offend.

To quit, you can't afford to
You know you'd get bored too
And this just can't be....The End.

My Grandson

I have a grandson with light brown hair
He has a few freckles here and there
He has the bluest of blue eyes
My grandson I quite a prize.

He has so many charming ways
He has also always made straight A's
He's tall, and slim and very smart
And has a tender, loving heart.

He's sensitive, and warm and kind
The sweetest kid you'll ever find
I and his teachers all agree
He's great in art and poetry.

He helps others when they're in need.
He also plants The Kingdom seed.
He's his Mother's pride and joy
A loving, caring, serious boy.

He's planning now to live forever
With a world of people who endeavor
To do God's will and mind His ways
And remain faithful all his days.

We Need Each Other

If you're too busy to help your brother
Forever will be a long time
If you're too hurried to help a neighbor
Where is the reason or rhyme?

We all need help at one time or another
No one can do everything on his own
If you're not there to help your brother
What happens to The Kingdom seed you have sown?

We all need each other, we can't be alone
Our unity holds us together.
So open your heart to ones crying for help,
No matter the time or the weather.

For help is the key to getting things done
You'll save others from worry and care.
Sometimes you'll find it is the mind
That needs the greatest share.
Sometimes it's depression that is the worst part
Being alone with no one to call
And all the troubles that break your heart
That steals you away from The Kingdom Hall.

So if you're needed, please don't say no
We all need the help of each other
Heed the call of one who's low
That's why we're called "sister and brother."

Pretty Little Cardinal

Pretty little cardinal glowing in the morning sun
The light reflects on red wings
A sight second to none.

It gives my heart a lift and it starts my day off right.
To see such loveliness as a cardinal in flight.

The Cardinal's Song

(pg. 21-- unsure of word in the last line; lift, light? of his song...)

When you wake in the morning
and it's cloudy and gray,
The song of a cardinal can brighten your day.
He sits at the very top of the tree,
and chirps away for you and me.

And when he flies from tree to tree
It's like he wants to share with me
The beauty of his glorious song
That slows my step as I walk along.

It doesn't matter if the skies are gray
The cardinal knows how to start my day.
I want to stop and stay awhile
For the light of his song, always makes me smile.

Love Gone Wrong

Love should be a beautiful thing
Like dew on the flowers at the start of Spring.
But all too often it begins to decay
Like the withering of petals, then he goes away.

Then heartbreak takes over and you cry with despair.
Wanting to hold him, but he isn't there.
You worry and wonder, why did he go?
Why did his love die? But you'll never know.

For love is a feeling you can't understand.
It isn't something to be touched by the hand.
Either it's there or it isn't, we'll never know why.
And the truly heartbroken, just lays down and dies.

God's Plan

God created man in perfection on an earth he
had arranged for man to live forever.
His purpose has not changed.
Though the first ones disobeyed him and
brought death upon the scene,
His son was sent to ransom man, his death would be the means.
That would bring mankind salvation and his prophecies fulfill.
His son taught all his followers that they must do God's will.
God's holy name they must make known
and defend him from the lies
that Satan told about him to destroy paradise.

Their faith in him they must maintain if they are to endure
to see the end of this old world and make their future sure.
Israel was God's chosen ones and was used by illustration
to show what God was yet to do for the peoples of all nations.

Now, we're told to take for us his name and witness for his right.
To rule mankind in righteousness, his word gives us the light,
it is the lamp that lights our way and tells us what to do,
if we're to live forever on an earth that is made new.

The Charm of December

December is here, there's a chill in the air,
Though the sun is shining everywhere.
It's cold at night, but the days are warm.
I guess that's part of December's charm.

When the temperatures start getting low,
Crazy people, like me, start praying for snow.
Yes, it's crazy, they say, that I must be
to pray for snow when I don't even ski.

But, I love to watch when the sunlight's beam
reflects on the snow like a diamond's gleam.
And the midnight moon on a snowy lawn
makes me resent a new day's dawn.

But December comes and December goes
with or without the glorious snows.
And when it's gone, January is here
and off we go with another year.

Beautiful Days

Beautiful days are whats in store
For the ones who survive God's holy war.
That war will sweep the bad away
and leave us room to work and play.

We'll have beautiful days from year to year,
and none who live will have to fear.
For gone will be the evil ones
With all their hate and greed and guns.

We'll have beautiful days to plant and sow,
And God's help to make our paradise grow.
Once again he'll bless the land
and bless the work of each one's hand.

Yes, beautiful days are whats in store
For those who survive God's final war.
So come and learn about his plan
To save this earth for perfect man.

Mountains

I love to lay in a mountain glade,
Or sit under a tree in the mossy shade.
And watch the birds flit from tree to tree
Dreaming of things that used to be.

The chipmunks and squirrels chatter and run
As they scurry about in the rays of the sun.
And if you're very, very still
They'll edge so close, it gives you a thrill.

I think of how it used to be,
When animals didn't fear man you see,
And how, in the future, it will be the same
Then we can join in their marvelous games.

Yes up in the mountains, you can see so much
With the sky so close you can nearly touch
and the stars at night, they sparkle so
And the full moon leaves an afterglow.

I love the mountains so near the sky
Where the leaves and moss make a bed to lie
And you can breathe the sweet fresh air
while you plan a future beyond compare.

Today's Problem

This violent age we live in today
shows the evil that led men astray.
Crime has risen at alarming rates
Why men even kill their loving mates.

They molest their children and rob their neighbor
They want "The Good Life" but not through labor
They sell their drugs and stockpile guns
In case nuclear warfare comes.

They look to science and political men
to explain the times we're living in.
They don't realize that it will take
Our God in heaven to alleviate
All the problems that plague mankind
And help us, Paradise to find.

So, don't wait until it's too late
To learn of Jehovah and the steps to take
To survive this system and it's evil ways
And to live in God's Kingdom, for which we pray.

Hear the Message

Are you listening to the watchman?
He has come to call us all
Out of Babylon The Great
And to the Kingdom Hall.

God gave them a commission
And Jesus leads the way
He guides them with their message
So we're safe on Judgment Day.

He is giving us a warning
And it's one that we must head
If we're to live forever
In a world that's free from greed.

For then there'll be no evil
Or men that's full of hate
It will be a world of beauty
This Paradise for which we wait.

Restoration

I sit by my door and watch the birds
As they come to my feeder to eat.
I enjoy watching them fly about
And hear their songs so sweet.

It's such a simple pleasure
But it's one most folks neglect
I find it helps restore my soul
From a world with no respect.

I have to cope with evil ways
As I do my daily chores
The peaceful birds help me forget
Tomorrow there'll be more

It gives me time to meditate
And calm my troubled heart
It also gives time to reflect
On what GOD's word imparts.

It helps to keep me close to GOD
His creations to admire
And realize it won't be long
Till evil will expire

Then we can live with no more fear
With birds and beasts together
To hear their songs and watch with joy
As we live on forever.

Hope for All

I love to watch the squirrels
As they run all around
Up and down the trees
And across the ground.

Their bushy tails flashing
In the glow of the sun
Always in a hurry for
There's so much to be done

They have to find their food
And store it in a tree
For winter soon will come for them
The same as you and me.

They have no one to care for them
And see that they're all right
They have to scurry here and there
And work with all their might.

But one day in the future
Man again will be their friend
And we'll all find joy together
In a world that has no end.

Listen to Wisdom

I love to watch the squirrels at play
They help me to enjoy each day
The same way as it is with birds
And all their songs that I have heard.

There are so many joys in life
That we could see, if not for strife
Most folks seem to ignore the plan
That God meant for perfect man.

That purpose though has never changed
And we find now he has arranged
To redeem man from all his woe
But to his son you have to go.

You must listen with your heart
To the wisdom that he imparts
And turn your path toward God's ways
To gain true life for all you days.

My Friend

You're the kind of friend I need
You make life worth living
You're so generous and kind
And always so forgiving

Even when I'm feeling low
You're there to help and guide me
I know no matter where I go
You'll always be beside me.

I Wonder

I just saw a bird
In a red stop light
Perched up there
So brave and bright
I wonder what
He was thinking about
When it changed to green
And the light went out.

The Mockingbird

The mockingbird sings such beautiful songs
And has such a large selection
It picks up the songs of other birds
And repeats them with perfection.

He chirps and chatters and warbles and peeps
And then he starts to trill
I stand and listen in wonderment
It gives me such a thrill.

I'm glad that I can stop awhile
And listen to his song
It makes the day more pleasant
Even though things still go wrong
For I can always pause and think
Again about the treasure
Of a pretty little mockingbird
Who fills my heart with pleasure.

My Prayer

Dear God,
I feel so guilty when I don't go out,
For I know you're the one I should be talking about.
But I'm getting old and full of pain,
It's hard to get up and face it again.

Please, God, don't give up on me
For I do talk to others informally,
You know we are imperfect brought on by Satan's curse
And as this old world lingers our problems just get worse.

Help us all to keep our faith and stay close by your side
And when destruction comes on earth 'neath your wings
may we abide.
Forgive us, please, when we fall short and stumble
in some way.
We need your forgiveness, It's one reason
that we pray.

We also give you glory for all that you have done
For showing us your mercy and providing your dear son.
He taught us of your prophecies of what the future brings
And how in these "The Final Days" he has become our King.

So bless us, Dear Jehovah and forgive us once again
For we love you and your dear son, through whom we pray,
amen.

Who Has Answers

There are so many problems in this world today.
Crime, disease, disasters all around.
Everybody seems to think they have the answers
But, really, only questions they expound.

Where, why, when, what if, these do not answer questions.
Most people do not know that book to read
The books written in this day just keep repeating questions.
They have no knowledge that will fill our need.

People know not where to look
And if you try to teach
They act as if they know it all
Their minds you cannot reach

They have been lied to for so long
They just don't know what's true
They lack the urge to study
So, they just lounge in the pews.

But the bible is the word of God
And it can set you straight
With just a little effort
Satan's lies can extirpate.

So you can learn the truth at last
And put down all objections
To the questions people ask
On how to get protection.

The bible gives examples
Of the many things we see
And builds within us confidence
That we shall be made free.

We Will Live Forever

Listen to the glorious things
God says that he will do.
He says "Death will be no more, I am making all things new."

There'll be no wasted areas
Seas, Earth or atmosphere
We know our God is truthful
His promises sincere.

We know we can depend on him
This world to cleanse from sin,
But first he wars with Satan
A war he's sure to win.

And then we'll live forever
On an earth that's free from hate.
It's one of peace and paradise
This Kingdom we await.

For man will reach perfection
In a thousand or so years
Then Satan will be gone for good
With no more need to fear.

Then God will be our Sovereign Lord
For all eternity
And we will live forever
In a world that's really free.

The Convention

We are attending a convention
Of Jehovah's chosen ones.
We have come to learn about Him,
And of all the things he's done.

He has promised he will teach us
How we can live forever
If we'll stay close beside him
And our ties we do not sever.

We must obey his will
And keep ourselves from sin
If we would conquer Satan
And the battle with him win.

Jehovah leads the way
With Jesus as his king.
He's fulfilling prophecies that
His new world soon will bring.

So, come and join our number,
There's another one next week,
And if you listen closely
You'll find the Paradise you seek.

Pure Language

Today is such a lovely day
The sun is warm and bright
We've come to hear Jehovah's word
His book is filled with light.

We know the light gets brighter
As the days progress
And as we see it more and more
We're filled with happiness.

It's such a thrill to see this light
The lamp that lights our way
It guides us to the fountains
That refreshes day by day.

So, help us please, to understand
The "Pure Language" we are learning
And let it build up in our hearts
The faith for which we're yearning.

Contrary to the Supreme Court
Regarding Life Support

They say that man should prolong life in any way he can
But, is it life, or is it death they prolong with this plan?
I do not think God meant for man to extend life uselessly.
He meant life to have a purpose, not be used abusively.

It really serves no purpose to keep such a one alive
For if Armageddon comes, would such a one survive?
Our courts should try and think things through before they take away
Our rights to rule our bodies and God's laws which we obey.

What makes them think that they know more than you and me?
Who gives them the right to prolong misery?
God gave to all parents the responsibility
To rule the lives of children with love and sympathy.

No one wants to see their child live on in endless pain.
What use when doctors say that they true life will no reclaim.
So, take these poor ones out of court and let them die in peace
For the Paradise that they may find is one that will not cease.

I guarantee when my time comes, if this decision I must make,
Take all your laws and life machines and throw them in the lake.

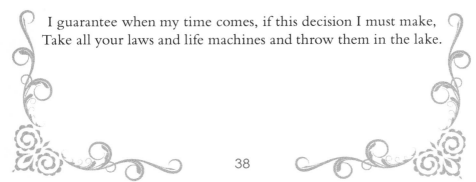

Emotions

Emotions control the way we live,
and all the things we do.
Emotions control the way we give,
and what we know is true.

When we're happy, things look bright,
When we're sad we see only dark.
When we cry it blurs the sunrise,
But a song recalls the lark.

So always keep your spirits up,
and pray to God above
That through it all we hold on to the truth
That the greatest emotion is love.

The Truth

I feel so sorry for the ones
Whose eyes are blinded from the Truth.
Those who miss the sense of it
Though they've heard it from their youth.

The preachers twist the word of God
Till it really makes no sense,
and when you ask them questions
They can make no sound defense.

They hide behind "God's Mystery"
That tells you they don't know
And even though they've studied
Their comprehension did not grow.

It is Jehovah's Holy Spirit
You must have to understand
The truth that is so simple
And the promises so grand.

Cloud Play

The sunlight playing on the clouds
Is such a gorgeous sight.
To stand and watch a sunrise
Gives a feeling warm and bright.

And then the clouds being to change
From red to pin to white,
And as the sun gets higher
It spreads it's morning light.

If you watch throughout the day,
It never is the same.
The winds chase clouds across the sky
As if it were a game.

And when the sun is going down
Pursued by wind or rain
We know that on the morrow,
We'll see them play again.

The Good News

Have you ever wondered why
The good news we declare
Has been veiled from the eyes
Of those who do not share

In the glorious beliefs
Of the coming Paradise?
It is the ruler of this world
Who has blinded their eyes

To the truth that's being taught
On how to save our lives.
You gain forgiveness that he bought
By having faith in Christ.

It is only unbelievers
That really cannot see
The glorious good news
That will set all mankind free.

For Jehovah gave his word
And his promises are true
But you must believe with all your heart
That all things will be made new.

The Art of Teaching

Talk to your children
Show them the way
Give them encouragement
Day after day.

Be sure to communicate
Aim for the heart
For teaching our young ones
Is really an art.

Talk to them early
Talk to them late
When you're in a hurry
Or when you must wait.
Don't pass up the chance
To teach them the truth
For Jehovah appreciates
The love of our youths.

Stay Awake

Stay awake and keep your senses
Don't give up and go to sleep.
There are still so many out there
That are Jehovah's other sheep.

Stay awake and keep on watching
For the season that is right.
Each season has it's harvest
When the fields of grain are white.

We must teach others this great truth
Stay awake and keep your senses
The time is here, you must decide
You cannot straddle fences.

So stay awake, keep working hard
The heart of all to reach
For the spirit of Jehovah
Gives us the strength to teach.

Red Moon

This morning as I stepped outside
The moon was shining bright
It was a red moon, round and full
Oh! what a gorgeous sight.

It really takes your breath away
To see the moon so red,
Especially since it's the morning sun
We expect to see instead.

But occasionally if we look around,
And in a new direction,
We see something like this moon,
An object of perfection.

He Takes Care of Us

A pigeon lights on my window sill,
And preens himself so pretty.
I wonder how they manage
To live here in the city.

Wherever do they find their food?
And where do they build their nests?
To survive in the world of brick and steel,
They surely must be blessed.

It goes to show how God takes care
Of his creatures large and small.
If we just put our faith in him,
He'll take care of us all.

My Brother

My brother's just got cancer
At the age of fifty one
He doesn't understand it's not
Because of what he's done

He doesn't know Jehovah
He's never listened to his son
He wants to rule his own life
And the truth of God he shuns.

He's never asked the question
What has Jehovah done for me?
He's like so many others
He thinks that he is free.

He doesn't know he is a slave
To Satan and his sin.
And until he recognizes God
True life he cannot win.

So when things, like this, go wrong
It's God they want to blame.
They don't know it's Satan's fault,
To charge God is a shame.

For he's given us the breath of life,
And all things that are good.
If only we would listen
And follow as we should.

Jehovah's Power

When the clouds are grey and black and tall,
And at anytime the rain may fall.
Do you get a taste of Jehovah's power
That can change it to sun or bring on a shower?

Do you realize he's promised too,
To change this world and make it new?
Do you recognize what he's already done
By sending to us his precious son?

Do you know that soon with Satan he'll war
And after that Paradise restore?
Then it won't matter if the clouds are grey
Nothing will take our joy away
For His name, for us, is a might tower
And we'll be protected by Jehovah's Power.

Jehovah Knows

Why are the winds being held back?
Only he knows why.
Why has Armageddon not come?
So many people sigh.

Why has Babylon The Great
Not been destroyed yet?
Do you think that God is slow?
Jehovah does not forget.

He's allowing time to separate
The dear sheep from the goats.
Jesus prophesied about this
His words we often quote.

Jehovah has the time set
And his schedule is just so.
Not one of the faithful will be missed.
Be thankful, Jehovah knows.

Speak Pure Language

Pure language is the truth of God's word,
We learn to speak together.
It builds unity among the ones
Who plan to live forever.

We all must speak pure language
If the sheep we would bring in,
And we must teach pure language
If they would conquer sin.

It means life everlasting
To learn about the one
Through whom God planned salvation
We mean Jesus Christ, his son.

We must learn from his example
And follow in his ways
If we would speak pure language
And to Jehovah give our praise.

He Loves Us

The trees and the grass,
And the birds that sing.
The sun and the moon,
And Everything.

All shows the love of
our God most high,
Even the pink
In a morning sky.

The clouds that play
And the rain that comes
Surely tells us
Who it's from.

Jehovah provides
A variety
Because he loves us
Don't you see?

The New System

A great new system will soon be here
We have Jehovah's guarantee
This old earth will soon be gone
And evil will cease to be.

Gone will be the governments
With all their lusts and greed.
Here and will be our sovereign lord
With all the things we'll need.

We'll have no place for evil ones
We'll have no need for money
For we have Jehovah's promises
Our land will flow with milk and honey.

Gone will be all illnesses
And there will be no death
Then we'll all praise God Jehovah
With every single breath.

Revelations

We pray to give Jehovah glory
For all the things He's done.
He gives us this privilege
When we put faith in his son.

Jesus came to teach about the Kingdom
And bring about salvation
Then after he went back to God
He gave us Revelations.

This tells us what he's yet to do
For people in our day
He tells us he will conquer sin
And Satan put away

It tells us how survivors
Will have a Paradise
Then there'll be a resurrection
Even unrighteous ones will rise

They'll have a chance to learn of God
And take their stand for Him
They'll have a chance to live forever
In a world that's free from sin
Then we'll praise our God Jehovah
For fulfilling all he said
And we'll have joy forever
As we welcome back our dead.

Persian War

This Persian War is part of Satan's plan
To destroy this earth for all of man
He knows now that he can't win
So he wants mankind in the same spot he's in.

To Saddam Hussein, Satan is no stranger
They're just like the dog in the manger
If they can't have it, then they'll make sure
That they ruin it for you and yours.

I cried when I saw the poor little birds covered with oil.
It's so absurd to take it out on Jehovah's creatures
They have no part in this war and it's features.

Saddam says "It's a Holy War"
But we know it isn't and what's more.
When Jehovah takes over there'll be no fear
For those who know "God's War" is here.

For he'll get rid of all the evil
And he'll make sure none of his people
Will ever have to worry again
For a Paradise they'll be living in.

The Wind

The raging wind is fearsome
As it blows so loud and wild
It makes me cower in my bed
Just like a little child

it makes my hair stand on end
And chills me to my toes
Where it goes and where it comes from
No one ever knows

It whistles round the windows
And moans throughout the night
You watch the trees thrash wildly
As you pray for morning light

When daylight comes
You look around
The effects can be seen
We know Jehovah uses wind
To help keep our world clean

Make It Through Each Day

A mockingbird is singing
In the early morning sun as it's coming o'er the hill
A new day has begun.

As I sit and watch the birds
And listen to them sing
I wonder at this world of ours
And what they day will bring.

Will it be joy and laughter?
Or maybe grief and tears
We never know what each day will bring
As we look forward through the years.

We only know that we must face
Whatever comes our way.
We pray Jehovah sends his help
So we can make it through each day.

God's Word

We must take time to meditate
Upon Jehovah's word.
We must ponder over his commands
And examples we have heard.

The Bible was written for our benefit
To teach us how to live
We must seek out our loving God
And appreciate what he gives.

Since the Bible was inspired by God
We know that it is true.
And by our study of God's word
We'll know just what to do.

If we are to please our God
And keep our worship pure
We must hold fast to all he says
And thus we can endure.

Paradise

Man and beast will live in peace
And the wolf will actually reside
With the lamb, and with the kid
The leopard will lay down beside.

A mere little boy will lead them
And lay down on a cobra's hole.
There'll be no more war and violence
The truth must now be told.

Nation will not rise against nation
And they'll not learn war anymore.
The human family will be united in love
That's what this earth was made for.

There'll be ample food and homes for all
You'll not ever envy your neighbor.
We'll work side by side building our lives
And it will be happy labor.

No more sickness and no more death
God will wipe out the tears from our eyes
No more pain or crying out
We'll be living in Paradise.

Jehovah's Gift

Hope in Jehovah and keep his way.
Do his will day after day.
He will exalt you to possess the earth
A gift intended since mankind's birth.

He'll take away this world of sin
And give us Paradise again.
He'll take away illness, death and sorrow
So we'll never have to dread tomorrow.

We'll live and love and worship him
And extend the Paradise we'll be living in
To encompass everyone who live
It's a precious gift Jehovah gives.

Read Revelations

Look, I'm making all things new.
Write, these words are faithful and true.
The prophets told us many things
About our God, our Lord and King.

They told how God will conquer sin
And the truth of how this world will end.
If only people now would hear
The truth will save them from their fear.

But, so many will not hear our word
The Bible says "At least a third"
They'll close their eyes and trust in men
To fight the war they cannot win.

For God is now our only hope
For answers men can only grope
We beg you now, read Revelations
It's our only hope for real salvation.

Lovers of Freedom

Lovers of Freedom, come hear the words
Jehovah is sending today
He tells us truth that we might hear
And from his path not stray.

He reminds us of his love for us
And why he sent his son.
He tells how Jesus gave his life
That our salvation might be won.

He asks that we tell others
Of all these promised things
Of his Paradise to come
And the freedom it will bring.

But also of the freedom now
That we really appreciate
And how we can make our freedom grow
By telling truths so great.

It helps to build our unity
By bringing in the sheep,
And makes the heart of our God glad
As our integrity we keep.

So stay awake and listen close
That you and your loved ones may see
How lovers of Freedom and sons of God
You may come to be.

Please Listen

Wake up, wake up, you must take heed
It's later than you think
You must give up this world of greed
The end will come as in a wink.

Don't while away your hours
As they did in Noah's day
Don't ignore the urgent warning
Please hear the words we say.

Jehovah sends his watchmen
To their warning please give heed
He always warns his people
So they know what they will need.

You must turn to the true God
To Jehovah and his son
They're the ones to battle Satan
And when that war is won
They will turn their attention
To the ones that followed him
To the ones that will not listen
And turn back from their sin

Jehovah's looking for the meek ones
That will listen now and learn
The ones who'll cleanse their worship
And make his kingdom their concern.

Yes, he's looking for the ones
That will make the great endeavor
To worship him with truth
They're the ones who'll live forever.

Fiftieth

It's your fiftieth Anniversary
Oh, what a lovely day
Your friends have all gathered
to honor you today.

We thank our God, Jehovah
For your years of wedded bliss
And on this Anniversary
Won't you seal it with a kiss?

Jehovah has helped you
In everything you've done
And we pray that salvation
To eternal life you've won.

You'll always stick together
Through wind and rain and sand
And we hope we'll all be there
To celebrate your year, one thousand.

Waiting

dedicated to my brother

I love you, Art, please understand
You're very dear to me,
And though your end is getting near
There is much more to be.

For after Armageddon
When you've come to life once more
You'll find some loved one waiting
As on a distant shore.

We know that through the resurrection
All death and pain will cease.
And then our loved ones will return
To find a life with love and peace.
He died a week later.

The River of Life

the river of life comes out from
God's throne
The blessings it brings are being
made known
The waters bring life and the
trees on each side
Will feed the many, they'll
be well supplied.

The trees will produce twelve
crops every year
All will be fed and we'll have
no more tears
The leaves will be used for
curing our ails
Of this we are sure for God
never fails

This water is pure and
crystal clear
It's there for all who are
sincere
In their search for God and
the truth he gives
And under his wings they
want to live.

So, please come and listen to
his word
Many things he has told has
already occurred
You can learn how to conquer over
pain and strife
If you'll only partake of
the river of life.

The Prize, Paradise

Paradise is going to be
The most wonderful place you'll ever see.
With plenty to eat and things to do
In a world that's free and fresh and new.

There will be peace as we've never known
And everyone will have a home.
The seas and the rivers and air will
be clean,
And the Earth once more will be lush
and green.

The waterfalls will glisten and gleam
And the sunlight will sparkle on every stream.
The birds will sing and bring us joy,
And the beasts will play with a little boy.

Jehovah will bless mankind once more
So, let's look ahead to what's in store
For all who work to gain the prize
Of living forever in Paradise.

New Light Bearer

I do all things for the glory of God.
I want to walk as his dear son trod.
Please help me to approach his throne
And work to make his divine name known.

To his throne I kneel and bow.
Please help me to keep my vow.
For forgiveness now I pray,
And I will strive to never stray.

One of his witnesses I have become,
And through his light the way I've won.
I pray his light I can help to shine
Then life everlasting will be mine.

All My Tomorrows

All my tomorrows belong to the one
That daily walks beside me.
I listen when he speaks to me,
And he's always there to guide me.

He holds my hand when I tremble
He comforts me when I cry
He promises everlasting life
If only I will try.

He smooths the pathway for my feet,
And gives divine directions.
Through all my tomorrows
He'll give me his protection.

So if I listen as I should,
And vow to never stray
Through all my tomorrows
He'll be there every day.

Welcome

Today is the first day of your Holy vow.
I'm so glad you're a sister now
You've come to Jehovah to do his will.
And with his help your vows fulfill.

Stay close to Jehovah and you'll
always be
As straight and as strong as the
mighty tree.
Like the limbs of the tree
learn to bend,
And you'll never break from Satan's wind.

Build your faith and keep it strong,
And he'll always be there if things go wrong.
But like the surf that caresses the shore
you'll have his love forevermore.

The Children of Jehovah's Witnesses

Our children don't lack anything
They are protected from many things.
They have our love and true protection
From this world and it's infections.

They don't join gangs or curse or fight.
They learn to love and do what's right.
They're taught the Bible through all seasons,
To understand the truth through reason.

They don't make decisions with pent up emotions.
Through study they build up faith and devotion.
They're not brain-washed or forced to believe
And they're proud of the understanding they achieve.

They don't take drugs or blood transfusions.
That saves them from Aids and this world's delusions.
They keep themselves pure for the marriage vow
That saves them from the guilt so many have now.

They don't have abortions, they value life
They're taught not to carry a gun or a knife.
They're taught to be nice and help their neighbors
They're taught to value the fruits of their labors.

We don't raise our children to live on welfare
They're taught to look out for others and care
For the ones that are old or weak or ill.
Teaching the Bible becomes quite a skill.

It teaches our children to communicate
And they are encouraged to meditate,
To channel their thoughts on things that are good,
And use the Bible for spiritual food.

This world would be a much better place
If it would heed what our children embrace.
Ask them, they'll tell you, they don't miss a thing
For they have Jehovah and Jesus Christ as their king.

Now, don't get me wrong, our kids aren't perfect.
We all fall short of that mark.
And some won't listen, but turn their backs
And walk away from the Ark.

And it breaks our hearts to see them go
For we know the prize they will miss
Is life everlasting on a Paradise earth.
What could be sadder than this?

The Superbowl XXVII

I couldn't afford a trip to the Superbowl,
but I still had a front row seat.
I watched alone on my TV
And saw the Bills get beat.

Of course I was rooting for Dallas
I've lived here for thirty years.
I've never seen a player like Emmitt Smith
I watched part of the game through tears.

It was the most exciting game
With Troy Aikman right on the money.
Novacek could do no wrong,
And Irvin's big play was a honey.

I couldn't sit still, I was jumping around
You'd have thought I was a child.
I've never been much of a football fan,
But Emmitt makes me go wild.

Harper came through like a champ again,
And Norton surprised every one.
Dallas walked away with a 52 to 17 win
And it looks like the Bills are done.

I'm glad I got to see this game,
It's the best all the Cowboys have done.
I know all the fellows are big, big fans,
But I'm a gal of sixty one.

The Crossing

What should you do when you are
Suddenly faced with death?
Do you cry or scream or faint
Or just quietly catch your breath?

Do you sit and try to figure out
just what you need to do,
To put affairs in order so they're
right when life is through?

You want to leave your loved ones happy
And hope they won't forget
How hard you tried to live your life
with nothing to regret.

It helps to know your crossing
Will only be a dreamless sleep,
With Jehovah watching over you.
Your memory he will keep.

And when you're resurrected
to the exegate elite,
To find your loved ones waiting
will make Paradise complete.

So, don't be sad when my time comes,
And try hard not to weep.
For you know I'll see you over there
with Jehovah's other sheep.

Banner

We extend our hand to everyone
We want to be your friend.
Our name is "Banner Finance"
And on us you can depend.

We want to help you if we can,
And we'll try our very best.
Just call your application in
And we will do the rest.

You need a little credit,
And a job and telephone,
And it helps if you've been a year
Or more in your present home.

We're rather proud of our record,
We've been around for thirty years.
We've helped a lot of people,
And we've saved a lot of tears.

So, if we can be of service,
We hope you'll come on down
Cause we take a lot of pride in
Being the friendliest place in town.

Great Day

How happy we'll be when that great day comes
When no one will say "I am sick".
We know it is coming, Jehovah has promised.
We just aren't sure of how quick.

It can't be too soon, we're all so tired
The new world will give us some rest.
But we know it will be in Jehovah's own time
For each must pass their own test.

We must listen and learn, to Jehovah must turn
To learn of the Kingdom so dear.
We maintain our faith and depend on our God
Through persecution and fear.

He sent his dear son to preach and to teach,
And show his disciples the way.
He gave his life to save all of mankind,
And we follow right down to this day.

So listen we must and Jehovah we trust
To thwart Satan and his lies.
Then with every breath praise the conqueror of death
And find peace in a grand Paradise.

Billie Joe (Brown)

I found a brand new friend this week.
And though we're tough as leather,
the battle we are fighting
seems easier together.

I try to keep her laughing
Even though she's feeling blue
And when I get discouraged
She knows just what to do.

We have a lot in common
We've talked "Of Mice and Men".
It's nice to meet somebody
And immediately feel such kin.

I know I'll be leaving soon
But I hope this bond won't end
For Billie Jo has come through
When I really needed a friend.

Doctor "C" (for Cold)

You're proud of your handiwork
You think surgery went fine.
But there's more to a good job
than making a straight line.

What it looks like on the outside
Isn't all that there is.
It's what's underneath that's
the meat of the quiz.

Were you trying for a record?
Is that why it went so fast?
Or did you just not care
that the damage was so vast?

I know there are surgeons
who specialize in nerve repair
It takes a little longer,
but it shows that they care.

We all know surgery
isn't going to be a song,
But by your indifference
you should not our pain prolong.

Do you think you have to be aloof
in order to do good?
Don't you know we need compassion
not someone who acts like wood?

I know you've just started
Like a flower you must grow,
But, take it from me, Doctor,
you've got a long way to go.

Thank You

I want to thank everyone for their
letters, cards and calls.
And let you know how much I've
missed the meetings at the hall.

You've helped me to keep my spirits up
and made me feel the love
That emanates from this hall
which is channeled from above.

For all the calls and visits
I will cherish them most dearly
And I hope this lets you know
that I mean this most sincerely.

But above all else I want to thank
Jehovah the most high.
For without his love and caring
I would have laid me down and died.

Just a Little Longer

Just a little longer and the new world
will be here.
Just a little longer, then we'll have
no need to fear.
For Satan's time is short, it's
nearing it's end.
Then Jehovah's Day arrives, on that
we can depend.

Just a little longer, oh, what a
promise grand.
Just hold on a little longer for
the Kingdom is at hand.
If it seems a little slow,
just remember we must keep
on searching for the rest
of Jehovah's other sheep.

Not one will be missed,
just hold on a little longer,
and if we seem to falter,
heartfelt prayer will make us stronger.

Stay close to Jehovah
and let Jesus lead the way.
Let us maintain our faith
and obedience display.

It takes much endurance
for things keep getting worse.
We need reminders from the Bible
please quote chapter, book and verse.
You help us understand
the prophecies so true
Only the faithful and discreet slave
can tell us what to do.

Our wait is almost over,
the prophecies are nearly done
And with a little more persistence
the prize we will have won.
So hold on a little longer
for the new world will be just,
And we'll all make it through
if Jehovah we will trust.

Joyful Work

The joy I get in doing my work
is a joy you can't understand
Unless you are here doing this work
With blessings from Jehovah's own hand.

I never knew that time in the field
could be so pleasantly spent,
Till I started working full time in the field
Now my joy by Jehovah is sent.

I feel I am doing the work of my King,
And I let him guide me each day.
I want to continue to follow my King,
for I know he is showing the way.

Yes, I get tired, but he refreshes my soul,
For the next door may be a dear sheep.
He wants us to keep searching for all the lost souls,
So, his commandments we faithfully keep

My joy is so great, I just want to do more
So I pray to Jehovah most high,
To let me keep on doing more and more
Till the New World on Earth does arrive.

For then we'll have joy teaching
those who return
The prophecies fulfilled by the score.
Then they will have joy
the ones who return,
To work for true peace and life evermore.

Your Wedding

Manuel and Sabrina
June 19, 1993

I came to your wedding
It's one Jehovah's blessed,
and with him in your marriage
it's bound to be the best.

Always let him be a part
of everything you do,
and though you'll have some problems
his help will make them few.

I know you'll always put him first
you and your loving wife,
and with his continued blessings
you'll gain everlasting life.

A Grandmother's Plea

I thought I had known loss before,
but this searing pain I feel
in finding hate has won your heart.
Oh God! This can't be real.

I walk the floor and cry with grief,
I don't know what to do.
I can't give up, you mean too much.
I must get through to you.

You were always such a happy boy,
and filled people with delight.
Now you're filled with anger, hurt and hate,
and all you want to do is fight.

The door was opened with hateful words
and Satan saw the crack.
Please listen, dear, I'm filled with fear.
We need you, please come back.

If hate and fight is what you want,
then recognize your foe.
It is Satan you much fight,
not those that love you so.

I'd lay down my very life for you
If you were to ask me to,
and there are so many others
that would do the same for you.

Don't fight us, please, we want to help.
It's your life that's at stake.
Don't let Satan be the winner
for Jehovah's heart you'll break.

And you'll break the hearts of all the ones
Who love you like a brother.
Forgive us all, and please come back.
Hear this plea from your Grandmother.

Help Us

Jehovah, help us through each day,
So many things go wrong.
Help us your spirit to display,
and always keep us strong.

Help us to rise above our ills,
and always put you first.
With your spirit improve our skills
So we can quench this thirst.

We must go forth and preach your word
For this is your command.
Without us truth would not be heard
and the end is now at hand.

So help us, please, to fight the pains
that we face every day.
For once your Kingdom on earth reigns
You'll take them all away.

Whose Work Is It?

It's not our work we do, you see
But the work of the most High Sovereignty
His purpose will be carried out
With or without our help. There's no doubt.

We pray to Jehovah to lead us to
The ones who are searching for this good news.
We depend on him to guide our feet
To the ones he calls "My Other Sheep".

Too often we forget who takes the lead
And how certain his plan is to succeed
He has his arrangements, designs and plans
And his way is not determined by man.

But, it's our great privilege to follow his way
To seek out the meek ones still living today
So get the right focus, it's his work we do
And the privilege of sharing is now offered
to you.

The Last Days

Men will be lovers of themselves,
to the depths of evil they will delve.
Lovers of money, self-assuming
Love of evil keeps on blooming.

Haughty, blasphemers,
without love of God.
Disobedient to parents
who spare the rod.

Unthankful, disloyal,
having no love of truth.
And the ones who are weakest
we fear are our youths.

Having no natural affection
in their hearts there is hate.
Not open to agreement,
just endless debate.

Slanderers, fierce,
without self-control.
Without love of goodness,
corruption unfolds.

Betrayers, headstrong,
puffed up with pride.
Lovers of pleasures
while God's pushed aside.

Having a form of godly devotion
But proving false to its power.
And from these God says "turn away,
take refuge in my great tower."

These are all signs of "The Last Days" of men
and the warning is certainly clear
The only salvation is knowledge of God
to his voice let us always adhere.

Death

You tremble in isolated terror
As you listen to night winds moan.
You're aware of the sounds of violence
As you cower behind bars on your home.

You feel hated, grieved and abandoned
As rage runs amok in the streets.
The wars of life surround you
Like an isle you're alone and unique.

Then comes a barrage of gunfire
And you huddle low on the floor.
You pray "Dear God, please protect me."
As bullets shatter your door.

When your path of life has ended,
You're forsaken by all those you know.
It doesn't matter how Death comes to call
You stand alone when facing this foe.

Dr. T (for Terrific)

One day this Doctor came in my life
And took it in his hands.
He did his very best for me
With carefully laid out plans.

He seems to care much more than most
I think it is his fashion,
And all the ones who follow me
Will receive his deep compassion.

He has a son named Andrew
Who is quite a handsome lad.
I hope when he gets older
He'll be just like his Dad.

I hope he won't mind telling his name
For I believe in setting things straight.
The one I'll always be most grateful to
is Doctor David Tait.

For all Who Thirst

Hey there, all you thirsty ones
You, who thirst for the knowledge of God.
Don't continue listening to their lies
Or sit in the pews and nod.

You must wake up and hear the truth
The end is getting near.
If you would survive God's Holy War
You must feel this Godly fear.

It's not a morbid kind of fear
But one that shows us how
To keep from displeasing our Most High God
By obeying his righteous laws now.

For learning his ways accurately
Is a protection for one and all.
It helps us endure these evil times
When this wicked system must fall.

So listen, please, the time is now
The warnings loud and clear.
No one but Jehovah can save our lives,
But <u>WE</u> must persevere.

Back to Back

Superbowl XXVIII
January 30, 1994

Back to back, you've done it again
The poor little Bills just can't win.
That's why the Cowboys are America's team
They know where they're going and
they're right on the beam.

The whole team was there, with Emmitt out front.
With Murray kicking field goals and
Jett booming punts.
Leon Lett stripped the ball from the pack.
Now, will everyone, please, get off of his back?

Aikman and Irvin, Williams and Harper
Taken all together there's no team that's sharper.
And I was so happy to see Bates on the line
I know he felt great to be playing this time.

But it still comes down to our favorite Smith.
The legs on that man is one of God's gifts.
So hang in there fellows,
you bring us much joy,
But what else can you expect from
The Dallas Cowboys?

Dustin

I know a little guy who is
as cute as he can be,
And I really do enjoy it
When he comes to visit me.

He has blond hair and big blue eyes
That really melts your heart.
He doesn't talk a lot yet,
But he's getting set to start.

You ought to see his eyes light up
When he hears something new.
He's really quite delightful
For a fellow not quite two.

I hope he comes to visit me
As often as he can
For I'd love to watch this little
one grow up to be a man.

The Critics

I've heard a lot about coffee
And drank it for fifty years.
The different stories they come up with
Just play on peoples' fears.

It's the same with many other things
Like popcorn, eggs and fat,
And then there is cholesterol,
Now, who came up with that?

But be careful to whom you listen
For the critics are not few.
Each one gets a strange idea
Then sets out to prove it's true.

And it really doesn't matter
If they do it honestly.
For all they're really trying to prove
Is that they're smarter than you and me.

So listen to whomever you will
If you think they'll give you a kick.
But as for me, it isn't the food,
It's the critics who make me sick.

Feelings of Winter

It's beginning to feel like winter
Grey skies everywhere.
The north wind will blow
And soon there'll be snow
and you'll cuddle in warm things to wear.

To some the days will be dreary
For the sun's lost it's warming glow
But the berries are sauced
On the windows there's frost
As the kids run and play in the snow.

There are diverse feelings for winter
It's cold, but there's warmth by the fire
You curl up in a chair
With your loved ones all there
And you feel you have all you desire.

The Changing Winds

The North Wind brings the cold and snow
As it whistles round our doors.
We put a rug across the crack
To block it from our floors.

The South Wind's soft and gentle
As it murmurs through limbs and leaves.
It's such a joy to open our doors
To a sweet melodious breeze.

The West Wind brings a darkening sky
With black clouds full of rain
And not til they've swept past our doors
Will we see the sun again.

The East Wind brings the morning sun
With clouds all puffy and white.
The robin sings outside our door
And fills us with delight.

The winds they come, and the winds they go
They bring things we love or we hate
If you don't like what they're bringing now,
All you have to do is wait.

Loneliness

Loneliness is like a dying tree
in the midst of a forest glen.
Standing there with no one to care
that it's plight is ghastly and grim.

In solitude I seek to recall
the waters that ran on apace
But try as I might there isn't a sight
for the passage has left not a trace.

In seclusion I think of the things I've learned
as I've traveled down life's long road
And I wonder why as time goes by
no one asks where the river flowed

So sitting forlorn and forsaken
I softly cry with despair
For when I'm all alone and all hope has flown
I have nothing left fut a prayer.

Jehovah's Commission

If you listen to what most people say
"All religions are good".
But do they follow Jesus' way
And practice it as they should?

Jesus spoke of Noah's day
This pattern would apply in the end.
Another great work would rule the day
And to his words we must attend.

Now ask yourself how many Arks
Was Noah told to build?
How many souls were on that Ark
And how would it be filled?

The Bible says there was just one
With eight souls who obeyed.
God told them how it must be done
Because his plans were made.

Thus Noah had a job to do
He didn't just say "I Believe".
He knew Jehovah would see him through
and his goal he would achieve.

Today, again, it's time for the end
Of a system that's wicked and evil.
There's just one truth, we can't pretend
That all will survive the upheaval.

So come and learn the Bible's truth
To refuse is a drastic omission.
It applies to all, both old and youth
To do Jehovah's Commission.

In Appreciation

to Anne McCaffrey

Your world of PERN
Is a world of delight.
It stirs our hearts
With it's strength and it's might.

The dragons and rivers
Are all so enthralling,
We're caught up in it's spell
and it keeps on snowballing.

Next came the firelizards
and we were enraptured,
Now you bring us the dolphins
and we're totally captured.

Once we start reading
the clock spins around,
but we don't notice time
we can't put the book down.

Sometimes we laugh
and sometimes we weep,
but we're so engrossed
we can't even sleep.

So, our greatest problem
all your fans are agreed,
is that you can't write
as fast as we read.

Brandon David

3-24-95

There's a blessed event
that has just taken place.
A handsome young fellow
with a sweet, charming face.

We're so glad you are here,
and now that you have been seen
we must admit you're the answer
to most anyone's dream.

The name you've been given
impresses us as just right.
"Brandon David" it is,
and it gives all much delight.

So, I'm sure you'll be happy,
and fill our lives full of fun,
for I know you will be
a really great, grand son.

Trevan, I Will Miss You

You are moving away
And my heart is breaking.
But all of my love,
and good wishes you're taking.

I love you so much,
And you know I will miss you.
But I think you should know
All the success that I wish you.

You will always be loved
Of that have no doubt,
But the love that you give
I just can't do without.

So please stay in touch,
And think of me often,
That will help keep me going
And the pain it will soften.

You're a young man now
On your own you must roam
But, don't let it stop you
From coming back home.

The Last Ride

She went out one day to ride away
and do some thinking alone.
She thought she could wander into the woods
and still find her way back home.

She rode for hours through sunlight and showers
before she tried to return.
But try as she might, it was suddenly night
and the trail she could never discern.

She rode all night, looking left and right
but never a path was found.
She would listen and then, she would listen again
but she heard nary a sound.

Now and again where the forest thinned
she caught a glimpse of the moon.
Then the snow did fly from a cold, dark sky
and an owl peered out of the gloom.

She was terrified on that long ride
and vowed if given a sign,
to never stray and wander away
to the land of the towering pines.

But she finally stopped and to the ground dropped
to huddle so cold in a glen.
And there she was found when spring came around
and carried home to her kin.

O.J.'s Innocent

Why go to the trouble to have a trial
if it's not going to clear his name?
Why take a year of his life
if he's still not free from blame?

Why don't you admit they jumped the gun
by trying to convict O.J.?
And messed up so much of the evidence
they let the real killers get away.

And notice I said "Killers"
For the deed was surely done
by two or more, I can't believe
that it was done by one.

There are many other reasons
I just don't have time to list,
and it really doesn't matter
the main point must not be missed.

That point being "O.J.'s Innocent"
and was cleared by the jury.
That's the way the system works
so even if you don't agree, don't be in a fury.

It's over now, O.J.'s free.
He doesn't need forgiving
He has the right to continue his life
with the freedom to make a living.

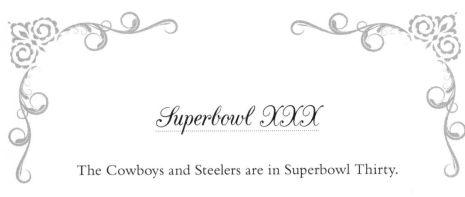

Superbowl XXX

The Cowboys and Steelers are in Superbowl Thirty.

Let's have a good game and don't play dirty.
Just go in there Boys and play to win
we have no doubts you can do it again.

Sanders caught the first long bomb,
then did his dance to cheer the Boys on.
Next Boniol stepped up and did his thing,
I guess that makes him the Field Goal King.

We're all so glad to see Haley back,
he came in and made the first sack.
Johnston made the fourth and one.
You can see these Boys are having fun.

Aikman had a good day in passing
and Irvin's catches were simply smashing.
Emmitt Smith was off and running
the way he moves is really stunning.

Novacek made the first touchdown,
then two interceptions by Larry Brown.
Aikman handed off two to Emmitt
He knew Smith could get in there to win it.

So, that's three Super Bowls in just four years.
Jerry Jones and Barry Switzer grinned from ear to ear.
It was a good game and though they make a few steam,
You must admit they're still America's team.

The Emmitt Zone

Do you know where is "The Emmitt Zone?"
He finds the place like it was his home.
He runs down the field on legs strong and stout.
They might slow him down, but
they can't keep him out.

How many times has he made that run?
Well over a hundred and it wasn't all fun.
There have been times when the going got rough
but our little guy knows how to get tough.

He lowers his head and digs for traction
You just can't keep him out of the action.
So no matter where our Emmitt may roam
he'll always find "The Emmitt Zone."

Grandma Would Say

When Grandma came in with something
to say,
Everyone snickered or turned away.
"Yeah, we know Grandma, we shouldn't say that."
Or Grandma would say "You should put on your hat."

Grandma would say "You ought to play nice."
Or Grandma would say "I can give you advice."
Grandma would say "Stay home boys, don't stray."
Or maybe she'd say "Let's bow now and pray."

But you wouldn't listen.
"It's the same old things."
All the sayings that Grandma brings.
Everyone knows what Grandma would say.

So, why do you miss her when she passes away?

I Miss You

I miss you when you're far away,
and remember little things you say.
I also miss you even though
it's only down the road you go.

I miss you each and every day.
So many times, so many ways.
I want to always keep you near
Your love is very precious, dear.

I miss you sometimes in the night,
and sometimes when you're still in sight.
I miss you all the time, you see,
if you're not holding hands with me.

Jehovah's Shepherds

Our brothers work so very hard
To see that we are served.
They shepherd us with loving hearts
and never are deterred.

It's sometimes hard to let them know
How much they mean to us.
As Jehovah's loving shepherds
We can turn to them with trust.

It's because they serve Jehovah
That we know we can rely
On the spiritual food they give us
In a bountiful supply.

So, dear brothers, may this message
Let you know how much we care
And how thankful all of us are
For each and every prayer.

The Four Horsemen

The Gentile times have ended,
for the Kings have had their day.
Our Christ now sits upon his throne
to lead us in his way.

It was in 1914 when they
recognized the sign
Marking the place where mankind is
in the stream of time.

That it is a sign is stated
in the book of Revelation
where the story of the horsemen
is important to each nation.

The first horse was white
and our King was on his back.
The second was a fiery steed
and to the earth gave sack.

The third was black and his rider
carried scales in his hand,
and as he followed the first two
brought starvation to the land.

The fourth horse was very pale
and on his back was death.
Hades followed close behind
to take one-fourth of mankind's breath.

Now, the riders are still riding,
but the ride is nearly done
And when the ride is over
then Salvation will be won.

Alternatives

We can go forward or we can go back.
We can have plenty or we can lack.
We can get well or we can stay sick.
These are alternatives that we can pick.

We can stay dumb or we can get wise.
We can plan ahead or be surprised.
The alternatives are up to each one
It all depends on what we've done.

We can save for the future or spend til it's gone
We can ask for help or go it alone
It all comes back to how we live
and we always have an alternative.

Gardens

There are gardens of lillies,
and gardens of roses.
Gardens we love
or where love resposes.

There are gardens we go to
to ponder or brood,
but a beautiful garden
can change our whole mood.

To work in a garden
refreshes our soul,
and we work even harder
if Paradise is our goal.

So, if we want a new Eden,
it's time that we start.
For our joy will be greater
if we all have a part.

Night Descending

The sun descends preparing for
the stars we see by night.
The sun declines from gold to amber
to the glowing reds of twilight.

Then the sky goes even darker
to a deeper purple hue,
and as the blackness now descends
the stars start to shine through.

I've heard that if you make a wish
on the first star that you see
it will come true, but though I've tried
it never worked for me.

Still it doesn't take a wish for
a full moon, round and red
to come over the horizon
telling us it's time for bed.

As we snuggle down to sleep
with the moon and stars above
we pray to sleep in peacefulness
protected by Jehovah's love.

I Want to See

I want to climb the mountain
where Jehovah's Kingdom stands.
I want to see the valleys
and the streams throughout the lands.

I want to see the animals
at peace with one another.
I want to be there at
the Resurrection of my Mother.

I want to praise Jehovah
with all my loved ones standing near.
I want to see the happy faces
with no one showing fear.

I want to glorify Jehovah
for setting mankind free.
And I want to see you all there
sharing it with me.

Turn Around

The long dreary days stretch out ahead.
You wonder, how long before I'm dead?
And will the depression get worse each day,
or will something come to drive it away?

It's sad when there's nothing to bring you joy.
You're like a child without a toy.
You sit and cry, but no one cares.
You wonder if anyone knows you're there.

You sigh, you don't know what to do.
You feel you have nothing to hang onto.
Then all of a sudden you think "What a Dope"
It's Jehovah that gives me hope.

He's there to ease the stress and pain,
and cleanse my thoughts like a gentle rain.
May I always deserve the blessings he brings,
and praise Jehovah as my heart sings.

A Trip to Fear

Have you ever traveled at your hearts command
Searching for a wonder land?
Once I tried, but went astray
and never again will I go that way.

It was like a line I couldn't break
A murmur that made my heart strings ache.
I couldn't turn loose, I couldn't exhale,
and when I looked couldn't find the trail.

The whisper I heard kept driving me on
All thru the night and til the dawn.
Even the wind seemed to hold it's breath
staying in expectation of death.

Then suddenly I began to shake,
and slowly the movement made me awake.
I sighed as the tears down my face did stream
and thanked my God, it was only a dream.

Memories, Good & Bad

There's no longer a flame
in my hear, just an ember.
All alone in the night
is when I remember.

Those long ago days
when our love was so grand.
We spent hours together
and walked hand-in-hand.

We played on the beach
and danced through the night.
We knew this was forever
for things were so right.

Then someone came by
and walked off with your heart.
She didn't love you
just thought she was smart.

But she couldn't hold you
she soon was to learn.
For the least little smile
would make your head turn.

Then off you would go
on another wild fling.
And you kept this up
till you lost everything.

Now, you're gone from us all.
We buried you in September,
but alone in the night
I'll still always remember.

Faithful Friend

There is nothing as great as a faithful friend.
A helping hand they will extend.
They listen to you when you despair
and offer all your woes to share.

They make you happy when you
are sad,
And join in the laughter when
you are glad.

When you need them,
they are always there.
A faithful friend is beyond compare.

My Daughter

When first I saw you after birth
I knew my purpose here on earth.
To love and care for this precious pearl.
Jehovah gave me this little girl.

I watched you grow and loved you so,
And taught you things you ought to know.
My life with you was tightly wound.
The joy you gave was without bounds.

When you were grown, you had two sons
My life as Grandma had begun.
How can I tell you the fun I had
Sharing our lives with these two lads?

You've made my life special in so many ways
I guess that's why I've lived so many days
The strength you've had has been there all along,
And with you beside me, has kept me strong.

So always remember how much I care
And how happy I am with the things we share
You are my daughter, there is no other
And I'm so proud to be your mother.

For Lena Bell

You're such a lovely lady
Your whole family thinks you're grand.
So on your 89th birthday
We think you deserve a hand.

So we applaud your long life
Which was granted from above,
And you've made it so much greater
By the abundance of your love.

Photo Gallery

B.J. Barkley

Daughter Tawnia and Husband

Trent grandson with wife

Grandson Trevan

My Mother

She's a woman which I admired a lot, and I loved her all her life.

My mother was not just my mom, she also was a friend, and my Spiritual Sister.

I remember she helped me through trying times when I was growing up, and her and I together working out each issue as they came.

She at many times had put me first, even before herself, teaching me to be a good person and mother myself having 2 sons later of my own and to 2 stepsons by marriage with my husband for near 30 yrs. Which with 4 sons and 6 grandchildren now ranging 20's to near 13 years in age. A wonderful big family I share now with my husband alone.

Losing 4 babies in her lifetime, I am very glad to be the one that lived and learned to survive from her love and care.

I loved my mother very much, I lived through most of her loses. Every year through the months that each death occurred, her heart seems to brake once more, sometimes I would cry with her, and in silence for her.

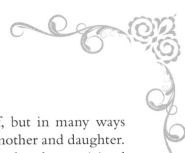

These steps in her life were brief, but in many ways grew closer in our relationship as mother and daughter. She was a fine teacher, Mom, friend and my spiritual sister, a sister in life growing up I didn't have (not that mom didn't try) as you know. We started studying the BIBLE with a couple as one of Jehovah's Witnesses. My mom and I found our eyes being opened for the first time to understanding the knowledge and answers from the Bible. We were looking for many years before, I know my mom since she was 14 years old, and I since the age of 12 years of age. Really it is like a light bulb coming on... Knowledge ringing truth from the beginning of our studies...

WOW, my life and moms really started improving so much through the years we had joy and happiness.

Truth being showed to us from the Bible. That helped us to view life with real hope all...

Later mom found out she had Breast Cancer, she endured treatments with help of myself and her grandsons. A year or so moving in with my husband and I. She continued writing all these many years of Poems to make her memories last forever. Mother passed on March 8, 2002. She fought her cancer for 11 years. Mom a sleep-in peace until resurrection. This book is to share her memories with all family and friends, and new friends to come.

CPSIA information can be obtained
at www.ICGtesting.com
Printed in the USA
BVHW031930111019
560567BV00029B/32/P